D1604805

Picture the Past
Life in a Sioux Village
Sally Senzell Isaacs

Heinemann Library
Chicago, Illinois

© 2002 Reed Educational & Professional Publishing
Published by Heinemann Library,
an imprint of Reed Educational & Professional Publishing,
Chicago, IL
Customer Service 888-454-2279
Visit our website at www.heinemannlibrary.com

Produced for Heinemann Library by
    Bender Richardson White.
Editor: Lionel Bender
Designer and Media Conversion: Ben White
Picture Researcher: Cathy Stastny
Production Controller: Kim Richardson

06 05 04
10 9 8 7 6 5 4 3 2

Printed in China

Library of Congress Cataloging-in-Publication Data.
Isaacs, Sally Senzell, 1950-
    Life in a Sioux village / Sally Senzell Isaacs.
        p. cm. -- (Picture the past)
    Includes bibliographical references and index.
        ISBN 1-58810-250-5 (hb. bdg.) ISBN 1-58810-415-X
(pbk. bdg.)
1. Dakota Indians--Juvenile literature. (1. Dakota Indians.
2. Indians of North America.) I. Title.
E97.D1 I78 2001
978'.0049752--dc21
                                                2001000497

Special thanks to Mike Carpenter and Scott Westerfield at
Heinemann Library for editorial and design guidance and
direction.

Acknowledgments
The producers and publishers are grateful to the following
for permission to reproduce copyright material:
The Art Archive, London: page 13. The Bridgeman Art
Library: Kennedy Galleries, New York, pages 1 and 10;
The Detroit Institute of Arts, page 27. Corbis Images: page
15; Bettman Archive, page 23. Library of Congress: page
7. National Maritime Museum, London: page 12. Peter
Newark's American Pictures: pages 3, 6, 8, 9, 17, 18, 20,
22, 24, 25. Werner Forman Photos: The Bradford
Collection, Buffalo Bill Historical Collection, Wyoming, USA,
page 19.
Cover photograph: Peter Newark's American Pictures.

Every effort has been made to contact copyright holders
of any material reproduced in this book. Omissions will be
rectified in subsequent printings if notice is given to the
publisher.

Illustrations by John James, pages 11, 14, 16, 21, 26, 28, 29;
Gerald Wood, page 30.
Map by Stefan Chabluk.
Cover make-up: Mike Pilley, Radius.

Note to the Reader
Some words are shown in bold, **like this.**
You can find out what they mean by
looking in the glossary.

ABOUT THIS BOOK

This book tells about life in a
Sioux village from about 1750 to
1800. It focuses on the group
called Lakota, or Teton, Sioux
who lived in present-day North
and South Dakota. These people
did not live in villages with
permanent homes. They were
nomadic. That is, they moved
several times a year to follow the
buffalo herds and to find fresh
grass for their horses.

We have illustrated the book
with photographs of Sioux that
were taken in the last 140 years.
We also include artists' ideas of
how the Sioux lived. There are
about 40,000 Sioux today in
North and South Dakota. Many
of them continue to follow the
customs of their families long ago.

The Author
Sally Senzell Isaacs is a professional writer
and editor of nonfiction books for children.
She graduated from Indiana University,
earning a B.S. degree in Education with
majors in American History and Sociology.
For some years, she was the Editorial
Director of Reader's Digest Educational
Division. Sally Senzell Isaacs lives in New
Jersey with her husband and two children.

Special thanks to Lisa Short Bull at the
Institute for American Indian Studies at
the University of South Dakota, for her
help in the preparation of this book.

CONTENTS

The First Americans

Thousands of years ago, people from other continents walked or paddled canoes to North America. When European explorers first arrived in 1492, there were two million people living in North America. We call them Native Americans.

There were three large groups of Sioux Native Americans. The Teton lived in the western Dakotas. The Yankton lived in the eastern Dakotas. The Santee lived in an area that is now Minnesota. The Teton moved from place to place. The Yankton and Santee lived in villages.

Look for these
The illustration of a Sioux boy and girl show you the subject of each double-page story in the book.

The illustrations of a **tipi** highlight panels with facts and figures about daily life in a Sioux village.

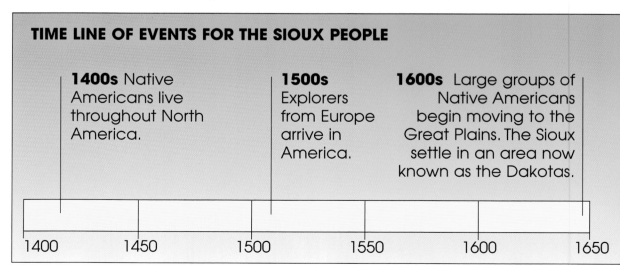

TIME LINE OF EVENTS FOR THE SIOUX PEOPLE

1400s Native Americans live throughout North America.

1500s Explorers from Europe arrive in America.

1600s Large groups of Native Americans begin moving to the Great Plains. The Sioux settle in an area now known as the Dakotas.

| 1400 | 1450 | 1500 | 1550 | 1600 | 1650 |

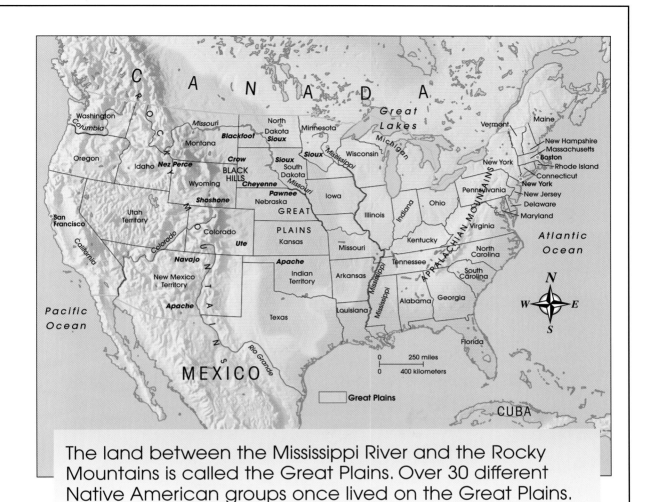

The land between the Mississippi River and the Rocky Mountains is called the Great Plains. Over 30 different Native American groups once lived on the Great Plains.

1779-1781 Thousands of Sioux die from smallpox disease brought by white settlers.

1868 U.S. government sets up Great Sioux **reservation** in North and South Dakota.

1650 Sioux begin using horses that are **traded** or stolen from other tribes or **settlers**.

1842 First wagons on the Oregon Trail pass through Sioux land.

| 1650 | 1700 | 1750 | 1800 | 1850 | 1900 |

The Sioux Village

From 1600 to 1800, thousands of Sioux Native Americans lived on the Great Plains, on land that is now North and South Dakota. They did not live in houses. They did not grow their food in fields. Their villages were more like camps with tents that they packed up and moved.

Each family lived in a tent, called a **tipi.** The whole village could be taken apart in a few hours.

The Sioux's main food was buffalo meat. The buffalo roamed the Plains. So the people moved their villages to follow the buffalo. In the spring, summer, and fall, the people sometimes moved every week. In the winter, they stayed in one place for several months.

Sometimes 50 families lived and traveled together. They settled near rivers, where they could bathe and get fresh water.

SPECIAL VILLAGERS

Each village had the following important people:

Chiefs – made decisions.

Shaman – helped heal sick people and explained the **spirit** world.

Warriors – fought battles with other tribes.

Crier – shouted out news about wars, hunts, and celebrations.

The Tipi

The Sioux lived in tents, called **tipis.** The women made the tipis from buffalo skins. It took about seven buffalo skins to cover one small tipi. The women wrapped the skins around a triangle of pine tree branches. The tipi could be put up and taken down in minutes.

The Sioux usually set up their tipis close together. They felt safer from enemy attacks. They kept dogs as guards and to help track small, wild animals.

Villagers often gathered outside a tipi. Inside the tents, the Sioux relaxed against backrests made of willow branches. They slept on soft buffalo fur. There were no beds or chairs.

A small fire burned inside the tipi. The women cooked there. The fire also kept people warm. Smoke from the fire drifted out of the tipi through an opening at the top. Each tipi had flaps to let in fresh air and sunlight.

Family Life

Children lived with their mothers and fathers, brothers, and sisters. Often their mother's parents lived in their **tipi,** too. No one lived alone. It was important to share food and work with other family members.

Each family had at least one horse. Horses were used for hunting and traveling.

Children had many playmates but also spent time with the adults. They were free to roam around the tipi village.

Girls married at about age fifteen. Boys married at about age 25 because they first had to prove that they were brave and strong in battles with enemy tribes. When a young man chose a girl to marry, he brought a horse or other large gift to her family. If her family accepted it, the wedding plans began.

CORRECT BEHAVIOR

If children did something wrong, family members took turns scolding them. The scoldings were embarrassing and children quickly learned to behave better.

The Spirit World

Everything in nature is alive with a **spirit.** That is what the Sioux believe. The Sioux treat animals, the sky, and the rivers with respect. If the spirits become angry, they may punish the people. The most important spirit is Wankan-Tanka, the Great Spirit.

SPIRIT NAMES

Sun - Wi
Sky - Skan
Earth - Maka
Rock - Inyan
Wind - Tate
Moon - Hanwi
Buffalo - Tatanka

Sioux warriors and chiefs prepare for battle by dancing around a fire and praying to the spirits for bravery and good luck.

The Sioux believe that the **shaman,** or medicine man, has special powers to understand the voices of the spirits.

Every summer, under a full moon, many tribes gathered for the Sun Dance. Men and women prepared for the ceremony but only men took part. They ate, danced, and told stories. It was a time to give thanks to the Great Spirit and to ask for good luck.

13

Lessons in Life

At the age of twelve, boys and girls prepared to learn which **spirit** would protect them for the rest of their lives. A boy was taken far from the village and left alone. He prayed and slept. He had to remember his dreams.

After four days, he was taken to the **shaman** to describe his dreams. The shaman could tell from the dreams which spirit would protect the boy. It might be a bird, a bear, or a star.

Before the boy was taken away, he prayed with the men inside a sweat lodge. Stones were heated on a fire. Then water was poured on the fire to make the air steamy. The hot steam cleansed the boy's mind and heart.

SPIRIT SIGNS

Once young people learned their spirit symbols, they used them throughout their lives. They painted eagles, lightning, or other pictures on **tipis,** war shields, and clothing.

A girl left the village, too. But an older woman stayed with her. When the girl returned, the shaman explained her spirit dreams. The villagers threw a big party for each boy and girl.

When a Sioux dies, the family places the body above the ground until it dries. Here, the body has been placed on a scaffold between the branches of a tree. The Sioux bury the bones in the ground. They believe the person will live among the spirits forever.

On the Move

The Sioux hunted animals for food. Without these animals they would have starved. When the people could not find deer, beaver, and especially buffalo, they moved to another part of the Plains. Within a few hours, the village women could pack the **tipis,** blankets, clothes, and kitchen tools. Dogs and horses dragged these things on a sled called a **travois.**

THANKS TO THE HORSE

Horses could carry heavier equipment than dogs. Now the Sioux could live in bigger tipis.

Until the 1700s, the Sioux had no horses. They walked across the Plains. Dogs carried their belongings on a travois.

A horse could drag a large travois. Without the travois, the horse was a very fast animal used in hunting and battles.

When European **settlers** moved to North America, they brought horses with them. The Sioux saw these large, strong animals and wanted them, too. They got horses by **trading** with settlers. They also took horses from enemy tribes. Horses helped the Sioux travel farther and faster.

A Child's Life

Sioux children did not go to school. They learned their lessons by working in the village and playing. Boys and girls learned to swim and ride horses before they were five years old. They also learned to hunt small animals with bows and arrows.

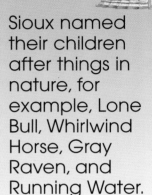

NAMES

Sioux named their children after things in nature, for example, Lone Bull, Whirlwind Horse, Gray Raven, and Running Water.

Mothers carried their babies on their backs in a cradleboard. This was made of wood and animal skin or cloth. The cradleboard in this painting has a bar over the baby's head with bells and charms to amuse the child.

At age six, mothers and aunts began teaching girls how to make **tipis,** sew clothes, and cook. Men taught boys to hunt and become **warriors.** Boys played many games to improve their skills. They held running races and horse races. They also threw darts through a rolling hoop. By age seventeen, boys were ready to join the warriors in battles.

Girls made dolls out of sticks and scraps of cloth. They made miniature tipis, too. This was all practice for the work they would do when they grew up.

19

Buffalo

Buffalo wandered freely on the Great Plains. **Scouts** from the Sioux village searched for the herds. Sometimes the scouts traveled many weeks. When they spotted buffalo, they hurried back to the village with the good news. The women packed the **tipis.** The men gathered the horses if they had any. The family headed closer to the herd.

FROM THE BUFFALO

SKIN: used to make shoes, tipis, clothes, blankets.
BONES: tools, toys, sewing needles.
MUSCLES: thread.
HORNS: cups and spoons.
STOMACH: pots.
RIBS: snow sleds.
HAIRS: rope and pillow stuffing.
HOOVES: glue, hoes, axes.
TAIL: fly-swatters and horse whips.
DROPPINGS: fuel to start fires.

These hunters are hiding under wolf skins, trying to get close to the buffalo. Where possible, they chased the herd over a cliff then collected the dead bodies. In these days, the Sioux did not yet own horses.

The women and girls set up the tipis while the men rode off to hunt. Young boys could ride behind the hunters. When the **chief** spotted the herd, he gave a signal. The hunters charged with bows and arrows. The chief signaled "Stop," when enough buffalo were killed. The Sioux killed only what they needed to live.

With horses, the Sioux could travel farther to find buffalo. They could ride faster to catch up with the buffalo to kill them.

21

Work and Play

The people were very busy after a buffalo hunt. Men and women took the skin off the buffalo. They cut the meat and cooked some of it for a village **feast.** The women dried most of the meat for eating the rest of the year. Drying meat stops it from rotting or spoiling.

This Sioux village is full of activity. Women are preparing buffalo skins, children are playing, **warriors** plan a hunt, while a young boy learns to ride a horse.

The Sioux made everything they needed. Men made knives, saddles, and bows and arrows. Women **tanned** buffalo skins to make soft leather for clothes and **tipis.** People also took time to play games and tell stories.

In this Sioux game, like lacrosse or field hockey, players hit a small ball across a field to a goal.

Clothes

The Sioux wore plain clothes every day. They had fancy clothes for special times. Women and girls wore dresses. Men wore shirts and pants in the winter. In the summer, they wore a simple covering that looked like an apron in the front and back.

The Sioux wore soft, slip-on moccasins for shoes. These moccasins are decorated with colored glass beads.

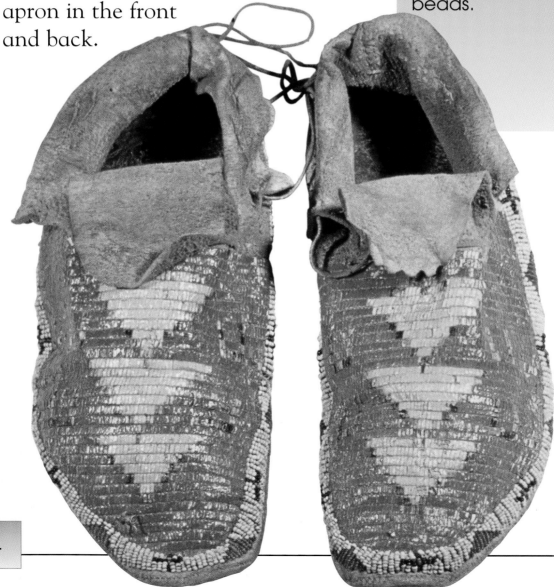

For ceremonies and for battles, **chiefs** wore feather headdresses and decorated clothing. This Sioux girl is dressed like a chief. She is holding a doll.

Women made all the clothes from soft animal skin, usually buffalo or deer. Men and women wore decorated clothing for **ceremonies** and **feasts.** They trimmed their clothes with feathers, porcupine quills, elk teeth, and bear claws. They used paints made from berries and grass. They bought beautiful glass beads from the white **settlers.**

KEEPING CLEAN

The Sioux took baths in rivers. They washed without soap or hair shampoo. Their hairbrushes were made of porcupine quills.

Food

In the spring, summer, and fall, men hunted animals for the meals. Besides buffalo, they shot deer, antelopes, bears, and wild turkeys. They trapped smaller animals, such as rabbits. Women collected wild berries, plums, and cherries. They also dug up wild potatoes and turnips.

Women cut buffalo meat into strips and dried it in the sun. When the meat was hard, they pounded it to a powder and mixed it with wild berries and melted fat. The mixture was called pemmican.

In the winter, the Sioux ate dried berries and vegetables. They ate pemmican, a dish made from dried buffalo. They also ate jerky which were strips of dried buffalo. The Sioux **traded** with other Native American groups. The groups who grew corn and beans traded them for buffalo jerky.

The Sioux prepared food in and ate from bowls, like this bowl carved from the wood of a maple tree. They cut food with a knife and ate using a spoon or their fingers.

Cooking

One way the Sioux cooked was by stone boiling. They dug a hole and lined it with a buffalo stomach. They put water in the hole, along with meat, roots, and berries. They heated stones in a fire, and then put the hot stones in the water. The water boiled and cooked the food.

MANNERS

A person invited to a **feast** would bring a knife, bowl, and cup. The person giving the feast did not eat until all the guests were finished.

At mealtimes, members of a family sat together in their **tipi**, cooking, eating, drinking, and talking.

Sioux Recipe—Wojapi

Along with eating animal meat, the Sioux also ate wild berries and roots. They got ingredients such as sugar and flour by **trading.** This recipe for a blueberry dish was a special treat for some Sioux groups.

WARNING: Do not cook anything unless there is an adult to help you. Always ask an adult to do the cutting and cooking on a hot stove.

YOU WILL NEED
1 small bag of frozen
    blueberries
1 cup (240 ml) water
1 cup (240 g) sugar
1/2 cup (120 g) flour

FOLLOW THE STEPS

1. Thaw the blueberries on the countertop for a few hours, or more quickly in a microwave oven.
2. Put the water and blueberries in a small pot over medium heat.
3. Add the flour, stirring carefully.
4. Stir in the sugar.
5. Stir continually until the mixture becomes thick.
6. Eat it as you would pudding, or spread it on crackers.

A Changed World

In the 1840s and 1850s, white **settlers** moved to the Great Plains. The United States government made the Sioux move to special land called **reservations.** Some Sioux fought against this. In the end, many of the Sioux died of diseases brought by white settlers. Others were forced to stay on the reservations.

Sioux **scouts** watch soldiers and **settlers** arrive on the Great Plains. The newcomers are interested in land, gold, and buffalo fur.

SIOUX TODAY

Today, thousands of Sioux live in the United States. Many want to keep the Sioux traditions and **customs** alive. They bring their families together for Native American **feasts** and parties, called powwows.

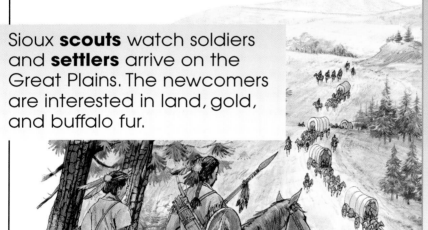

Glossary

ceremony special way of marking an occasion, such as a wedding ceremony

chief one of the leaders of a Native American group. Chiefs were chosen because they were brave and generous.

crier person who shouts out news

custom special ways of doing things

feast large meal for a lot of people, usually to celebrate a happy event

reservation area of land set aside by the government for Native Americans to live on

scout person who knows the land well and travels ahead of others to look for buffalo, rivers, or enemies

settlers people who make a new home in a new place

shaman person who understands the spirit world and has powers to cure illness

spirit part of a person or animal that holds feelings and thoughts and which cannot be seen or touched

tan way to turn animal skin into a soft material for making clothes, blankets, and tipis

The flesh was scraped off with stones, bones, or metal tools. Then the skin was softened by rubbing it with animal brains.

tipi cone-shaped tent made of animal skins

trade to exchange one thing for another

travois type of sled used to carry things. It is made with two long poles that are connected with leather or a net.

warrior someone who fights in battles

More Books to Read

Kavasch, E. Barrie. *Lakota Sioux Children And Elders Talk Together.* New York: Rosen Publishing Group, 1999.

Lund, Bill. *The Sioux Indians.* Danbury, Conn.: Children's Press, 1997.

Index